Sharks in the Rivers

Also by Ada Limón

Sharks in the Rivers

Ada Limón

milkweed
EDITIONS

Published 2010 by Milkweed Editions
Printed in the United States of America by Kingery Printing
Cover design by Jeenee Lee
Cover art by Stacia Brady
Author photo by Jude Domski
Interior design by Connie Kuhnz
The text of this book is set in Minion Pro
22 23 24 25 26   15 14 13 12 11
Second Edition

Please turn to the back of this book for a list of the sustaining funders of Milkweed Editions.

Library of Congress Cataloging-in-Publication Data

Limón, Ada.
     Sharks in the rivers / Ada Limón. — 1st ed.
          p.   cm.
     ISBN 978-1-57131-438-3 (pbk. : acid-free paper)
     I. Title.
     PS3612.I496S53 2010
     811'.6—dc22
                                        2010007362

This book is printed on acid-free 100% post-consumer waste paper.

for Ma, Cynthia, & my lovelies

(The Insides)

1.

2.

Sharks in the Rivers

What matters is this: void. The world alone. The river's mouth.

—Federico García Lorca

1.

Oh, I used to dream of oceans and streams,
flowing and growing strong.
Where have all those days gone?

—The Black Keys

Sharks in the Rivers

We'll say unbelievable things
to each other in the early morning—

our blue coming up from our roots,
our water rising in our extraordinary limbs.

All night I dreamt of bonfires and burn piles
and ghosts of men, and spirits
behind those birds of flame.

I cannot tell anymore when a door opens or closes,
I can only hear the frame saying, *Walk through.*

It is a short walkway—
into another bedroom.

Consider the handle. Consider the key.

I say to a friend, how scared I am of sharks.

How I thought I saw them in the creek
across from my street.

I once watched for them, holding a bundle
of rattlesnake grass in my hand,
shaking like a weak-leaf girl.

She sends me an article from a recent *National Geographic* that says,

*Sharks bite fewer people each year than
New Yorkers do, according to Health Department records.*

Then she sends me on my way. Into the City of Sharks.

Through another doorway, I walk to the East River saying,

Sharks are people too.
Sharks are people too.
Sharks are people too.

I write all the things I need on the bottom
of my tennis shoes. I say, *Let's walk together.*

The sun behind me is like a fire.
Tiny flames in the river's ripples.

I say something to God, but he's not a living thing,
so I say it to the river, I say,

I want to walk through this doorway
but without all those ghosts on the edge,
I want them to stay here.
I want them to go on without me.

I want them to burn in the water.

Flood Coming

The pulled-apart world scatters
its bad news like a brush fire,
the ink bleeds out the day's undoing
and here we are again: alive.

The tributary of this riverine dark
widens into the mind's brief break.
Let the flood come, the rowdy water
beasts are knocking now and now.

What's left of the woods is closing in.
Don't run. Open your mouth big
to the rising and hope to your god
your good heart knows how to swim.

The Widening Road

All winter the road has been paved in rain,
        holding its form as if made of its own direction.

We have a lot of these days. Or not.

A woman in a car staring out, her hands going numb.
        When did the world begin to push us so quickly?

A blue jay flies low over her into the madrones.
        She can still see it—its bright movements rocking a branch—
        surely delighted that it matches the sky.

The honest clouds.

A tenderness grows like a fluttering in her hand.

She wants to hold it in her arms but not pin it down,
        the way the tree holds the jay generously
        in its willful branches. The spring is blowing
        through her, pulling the dead debris free from her limbs.

She cannot decide what she desires, but today it is enough
        that she desires and desires. That she is a body

        in the world, wanting, the wind itself becoming

        her own wild whisper.

Good Enough

To be utterly lost is a fine story
(good enough), especially in some small creeks
in the gold madrone world I came into.
To hide underneath Highway 12,
and listen to the automobiles go by while I,
another creek-thing (good enough), go marching
in the morning current, older than I remember
(good enough), a little better for wear (good enough),
a little less shiny and new (good enough),
a river rock with ten thousand waves upon it,
ten thousand perfect (good enough) bruises.

High Water

We become our own land sometimes,
        no important nation, the hand on our door, the ship mast come
up over the flat ocean of dishwater.

Say there is nothing to it; my rock is your rock, my empty name
is your empty name, but mine reminds me more of me.

If we begin to count our blessings we could cull up the very stones
and bones in the pavement, but we'd never count the dust.
        We distrust what we become.

One woman stands in the middle of the street and looks both ways
for a long time, until she continues to walk that yellow line straight
        into the river.

Bless our own kingdoms, our thrones of maps and mirrors.

Perhaps the woman believes she can walk on water,
or that the road is just the river deadened by factories and footprints.

In 1890 her grandmother lived at the very edge of town, and all
        around her the marsh hawks sat low in the reeds.

She sang, *Loo-rye, loo-rye, loo-rye, loo,*
because she thought it was the sound the river made.

        And no life is as long as a river.

At dinner we have a discussion about acceptable behavior—
how nothing feels quite right this winter.

She walked straight into the river! Must have thought she was Moses!

And on the ride home I grab your hand on the stick shift
and want to say, *Insanity feels closer to home
than here sometimes*, but instead

I point to a white sign on a building that reads,

If you lived here, you'd be home by now, and smile, *Isn't that true?*

And they haven't found the woman's body,

twelfth day of rain, creeks flooding high over highways,

white water makes the road a living river.

And when we're home I stand in the street a bit.

Then we sing, *Loo-rye, loo-rye, loo-rye, loo,*
because we think it is the sound the river makes.

　　And no life is as long as a river.

Diagnosis: Even the Stillaguamish River Cannot Stop Time

Your cat has dragged a dead bird onto the porch again.
Fragments of its dull wings still hang in the air, the real live
wind brings a cold rain up from the Sound. Your hands
are wet; time moves too fast. Things were easier earlier,
when the Snow Goose was open for business and the sun
lay its original light all up and down the Stillaguamish River.
Everything, now, is an interrogation. *Why this bird? Why
this interruption, soaked to the bone?* The river is still there—
steady and cunning with current. It does not answer,
but it loves the conversation; it is both the cat and the bird.
It is at once your body dissolved in this rain and your
beautiful wet hands trying to hold onto water.

Rescue Animals

Round the mountain and we've entered
a no-man's-land of earthward and fallen.
Barn owls wake the sky and set the world
bursting, white-faced and beating. Your
cold hands carry the flashlight, and mine
the key, always the key, for safekeeping.
I'm telling you about the animals: the egret,
the goat my mother rescued, the orphan
goose, the blind quarter horse, the bullfrogs,
and you're watching where we're stepping
so carefully, so seriously. I'm pointing out some
stone I love and I know I sound ridiculous,
my voice like too-loud chimes in a windstorm.
Your head is bowed and all your life
you've wanted to know some place like this
existed and, for a moment, your lost face
belongs in the barn, rushed in from the city's
traffic-hounded concrete, limping here
out of wounded whimper. So, I keep you—
lost and found—surrounded by the sweet
barbed wire of tumbled limbs until you are
tough enough to kick through the gate, break it,
knock over the water trough and go mean-wild again.
I think I've been standing in the barn door
for days, or perhaps for one long year,
filling the still-full food bowl and leaving the stall
piled with blankets, but tonight I want you
never to return. Tonight, I miss only those
stones I owned, that long cold walk in the dark
when no one's watching, when no one needs
to force my footstep further—or even
hold me back from falling.

Spawning Ground

Soon, the ice comes, the pinch of frozen
particles entering the mind's white slate.
I write my own name in the snow; it says,
Dead Bird. I write yours and it says,
Possible Rope. Your mouth is in my
pocket. A chum salmon crosses
the Skokomish Valley Road and flips
into a drainage ditch. It's perfectly happy
in the small, dark, eelgrass world.
I envy its silvery body, so sure
of its singular want. I write its name
in the snow; it says, *Provide Passage.*
It says, *My World Keeps Opening—*

This Practice

They say the first thing that goes
is short-term memory. We forget
our keys, we forget the address,
we forget the name of the president.
I like to think it's just a matter of practice—
we've had more time to practice the memory
of our brother's face, our favorite light,
the creek that runs down the center of town.
I want to practice. Like the Russian soldier
who had to make up a word to say how
hard he would fight, said he would fight
fiercefully, that's how I will remember you,
how I will practice—*fiercefully*.

Paseo del Bosque

I saw myself by the Rio Grande watching
    a crane swoop down over the collection pond.

I was the fish in the drainage ditch,
    you, the crane's scissoring shadow.

There are whole areas of that river where you can still hear drumming.

There is a group of trees you can walk in
    and say, *People live here.*

When we met I was too young to walk—
    I wore a button that said, *Boys are a Piece of Cake.*

I had a dream I was surrounded by butterflies—
              until they stung me over and over.

    I woke up and had the word *mariposa* in my mouth like bad water.

I saw myself on the river's edge, sinking in the rapids,
    the brown water like liquid clay.

    I was under the cottonwoods forever.
    I was under the sage bush like a stuck bird.

I heard you could take the sand from a red anthill,
suck on the grains and put them back wet.
        The ants would carry your worries away.

Everyday I put more sand in my mouth,
and everyday I woke up with a buzzard outside my window.

I have done my duty here. I have sucked my own mouth dry.

I am the only ant carrying my own sand—
and it's too heavy even for the current of the Rio Grande.

Body of Rivers

The river comes to the body bold,
dreaming of black hues and a gestured
cluster of colored fish. This is the way
the world runs through us, its instruments of moon-
water and hangnails of hope. River, river,
listen, I understand the urgency. I am
floodwater running; I am dirt ditch rising.
A constant glutton for the outpouring pond,
I am trying desperately to return to gone.

Not Enough

Load me up with stones, can you
see my body twisting?

    All along this road there are both brave
and buried bones, here, and here, and one

in my dirt-filled heart.

To be the General of Sorrow, the grave
    meanness of a walk into one's own memory.

How does one lay down her
    rigid plans for infinity?

Like a sword in the street? Take it, do with them what you will.

There is no *other* here, except for me,
          no lonely pendulum, no
      swing me to the middle of the crowd.

Look at us, our selling selves in the world again,
    committing to this orbital mess.

What is the curve, the horizon meeting my shoulders?

Where does the curve end?

I told a friend last night that I thought it would be a plane crash,

    one blazing bird tumbling me to the next hand.

He says—his sight half-gone,
another silvery operation after another—
    Not me, I go pecked to death
by a hummingbird slowly, inconceivably torn apart.

This is how we turn, so rotated and spun
in our own isolations.

The end is a circle, it comes again, and again.

Do not erase me.
(Yes, we say it.)
Do not erase me.

The path is forgotten, but we are still walking;
we whirl out our limbs to the defeated world,
this city's tiny blue welt of sky,

say, *We're molded in metal here together,*
we contend with catapult, we will stick
this spun-surly life out. Towering in our blooming
darkness, our bodies of bronze and blood,
our end still ending, our reach
only missing and missing the door,
we still keep walking, we still ask for more.

Overjoyed

What's the drunk waxwing supposed to do
when all day's been an orgy of red buds
on the winery's archway off Gehricke Road
and it's too far to make it home, too long
to fly, even as the sober crow goes. What's
the point of passion when the pyracantha
berries keep the blood turned toward
obsess, obsess. Don't you know those birds
are going to toss themselves to the streets
for some minor song of happiness? And
who can blame them? This life is hard.
And let me be the first to admit, when I
come across some jewel of pleasure, I too want
to squeeze that thing until even its seedy heart
evaporates like ethanol, want to throw my
bird-bones into the brush-fire until,
half-blind, all I can hear is the sound
of wings in the relentlessly delighted air.

Territory

Every one of us has a sparrow
underneath her tongue,
bouncing back and burrowing.

On the crest of a spared mountain,
we can barely say, *Sleep well,*
to the full night of open obsidian and owls.

We long gone tree-leaners
raised on poison oak and poppies
make our way to the creek bed.

We come to lie down again,
our flightless selves in the river rocks,
to bear witness.

What impossible longing.
Black oak and manzanita looming
in the nest of this natural home.

Cowbird and grackle, black phoebe.
Every one of us with a bear inside
(a scorpion, a rattlesnake).

Our danger is calmed
by our watermelon sun,
by instinct.

(Acknowledge the dirt
beneath us, expect nothing.)

We are vine and hummingbird,
eucalyptus root and centipede,
junco and blue-belly lizard.

(And sometimes the drowned deer,
and sometimes the trapped opossum,
the wayward dog, the wayward dog.)

But a little tree dust on the mountain
and the chest finds its bird again,
laughing loud on its juniper and wisteria.

And listen, even we non-fighters
know what a precious territory is
when we see it. Soon, we'll say,

Tongue-sparrows, flinting
like well-carved arrows,
fly into the yellow foxtail

and rye we were raised on.
Alluvial soil, this claim we call
our own, take us back in.

The Barer the Bones

Centered in the streets
under clouds of miscalculation,
I'm taking off my creature-drapes
for the record. The primary
animal is not as upset as
the one we are told to be
(the electronics we are tied to—
our sudden lack of atmosphere).
Be a doll and get the door,
remove the cross from its hinges.
The mountains are all gone
around here, all done and gone,
even the sea is trapped in a plastic
bag stuck in a tree, some flawed
trash-bird we have made
of our own poor boredom.
Let's go find the unusualness,
the great giant wonder,
the lasso that brought down
the last remaining metal mean.

2.

I would leave it alone if I could leave it alone.

—The High Strung

Crush

Maybe my limbs are made
mostly for decoration—
the way I feel about
persimmons. You can't
really eat them. Or you
wouldn't want to. If you grab
the soft skin with your fist
it somehow feels funny,
like you've been here
before, and uncomfortable
too, like you'd rather
squish it between your teeth
impatiently, before spitting
the soft parts back up
to linger on the tongue
like burnt sugar or guilt.
For starters, it was all
an accident; you cut
the right branch
and a sort of light
woke up underneath,
and the inedible fruit
grew dark and needy.
Think crucial hanging.
Think crayon orange.
There is one low, leaning
heart-shaped globe left
and dearest, can you
tell, I am trying
to love you less.

The New World of Beauty

Beauty in its optimal world,
denies all its adversaries,
        says, *Boo*, says, *Who's there?*

        And the ugly parts scatter.

When I met you, you had a boxer's body
    and a mug to match your bruises.

You complained about the heat,
        the small rooms, so stifling.

Gringo, with your hat to block out the world,
        come a little closer.

There's a lion in a cage,
        a lion in infinity (in here), pressed up against the bars.

It's got it worse than you.

        Don't think about Laika in orbit.
        Don't think about cringe and catastrophe.

There's a lion in a cage
        just outside of Ensenada. Poor yellow beast,
in the desert of Cataviña.

His heart has been lost and
        already prepared for dust.

        Say something pretty about it. I dare you.

Something pretty. (Break it.)
Something pretty. (Kill it.)

Beauty will come to you, lay down at your feet,
   put its wild hair in your lap.

Will you know it, Gringo?

The Russian River

In the 1973 Ford LTD, we took Highway 12
and headed toward the wide Russian River.
It was the summer of our final year of high school;
we were all so stoned that the world was perfectly defined
by goodness and realness and the opposite of those.
It was 98 degrees and even with the windows open
it was hard to breathe. Outside of Guerneville
we found the party—beautiful bodies jumping off
the cliffs into the deepest part, a raft of natural
naked women floating like an old cigarette ad
down the current. I was going to marry you.
Hours into the afternoon we swam to each other
and walked upriver. I remember thinking this
was what life was, and what I had always wanted:
being pressed on a warm, flat rock, our wet imprint
there as if it would matter, *I am holding on. I am holding on.*

Marketing Life for Those of Us Left
—For Jess

Stuck in the answer of day,
all we've got are these people to rely on—
and trees, and the grasp of a river in the mind.

High hillside of home,
I'm waving from the cement center, can you see me?

All the beautiful girls in the office are laughing and I laugh
along. And all of us good people, honest and clean,

and what puts the mean in some of us?

Sumptuous mountain, midnight milkweed,
come to the valley of neon and no-crying.

I've got this big city in me. Pretty on fire, pretty high-wired.

It's been a year since Jess died; she said,
I always knew it would come down to pills in the applesauce.

And the house is not haunted, nor the office.

I wish they were, don't you?

We were wilder before—see-through shirts
and model boys and bouncers in hotel lobbies
across the country.

Who knew it would be hard to live to thirty-two?

A friend says the best way to love the world is to think of leaving.

We're all in trouble, you know?
Piles of empty stars we've tossed aside for the immediate kiss.

Push me around a bit, shake my pockets, I store everything
in my mouth. I'm going to make an apple out of plastic,
going to make a real star out of the apple, then
I'm going to sell it to you.

I'm going to tell you it's the most important thing.

I'm going to tell you I'm sorry, I'm going to crash
on your communal couch of unwanted.

Let's say bloom.
Let's say we're a miracle of technology.
It's harder not to say anything.

It's all we've got, say it, pinch me.
You're here. So am I. So there.

Good Girls

Some rivers flow to the ocean. Some don't—
or seem like they don't. Stubborn little girls
with their hands in their pockets going straight
through the ground. Under all of Skagit County,
under all of Nooksack, they sneak below in dirt
like guilty tricksters, poor black-hearted river,
poor desperate go-er. And the boys!
There on the road, holding a cattail or
some watery mess of weeds and worms,
the boys worry about where their good gal went,
their one faithful dear disappeared.

Hardworking Agreement with a Wednesday

I have an agreement with the day:
I won't talk too much.

I won't be the most complicated minute in its
configuration of hours.

Come to the office with me. Stay awhile.

The woman in the elevator (who's in sales) is so nice,
but she says my name over, and over, and over.

(Even when I don't say hers.)

She says, *Good morning, Ada.*
How was your evening, Ada?
Have a good day, Ada.

So my name becomes an advertisement, or a product
to be bought and sold. I want to take it back from her mouth.

I cannot stop looking at the bird out the window.

We've named him Stanley. He's half-angry,
half-slow, half-bird. One-and-a-half figurine.

I want him to live somewhere else, but it's not my decision.

He likes the rooftop of the high-rise,
the hot soft tar grasped in his claws. He likes the danger.
He likes the dirt on his beak. He likes it rough.

I want his flight to be my own,
as if wings themselves could be willed.

Let's fly south to Monterey, to water, to ether, to air.

Everything is off-limits.
Everything is unreal.
Everything is lament and let go.

Dear Today,
I have said too much, yet give me this—
I want to be a physical doll, just for now,
a stupid, splendid thing,
tumbled into the touchable day.

Homesick

In the Glen Ellen night, banned to the backyard
for running in the house, I and a particular tree
became fast friends in the green sequined summer.
I situated myself inside it, where I watched
the yellow of our kitchen window—my
soundproof family. I liked the shadows cast
in gobo-leaf prints on my bare limbs. I imagined
myself growing green sprouts and maroon bark
that shot into the dirt. Today in this terrible
cement city, I will do this bidding, but I tell you:
I am there, across from Sonoma Creek, still hidden
in the tree, where I cannot be unbelieved.

How to Give Up

Someday, unbeknownst to the sorry
lot of the dark virile ghosts in your corner,
the blue moon will actually come.

Bruised by the stone glare of the limelight,
it'll come to stand in your tenuous doorway,
ready to admit it's been late in coming.

Leave the indolent lotus-eaters right
then and there, their gorgeous blond faces,
and go to work, your shoulder to the hard sky.

Stop blaming the heat, the weather is
not a response to your desire, or non-desire,
you are part weather, part flower-leaf waving.

Lieutenant of the present room, practice
more of those human blunders, less fast lies,
leave your fumbling empty to the glossies.

You can be taken down as easily as taken up,
leave your arms loose in the hour, your body
buoyed by your own coalition with the air.

The Crossing

—For Cynthia

We drive up to Smokey Point
    and the Snoqualmie River is muddy.
The fish have been crossing for days—
    all night, the news of coho
crossings—sightings of those swimming
    beaming finners.

One band of sun holds its hands
    down on the field, but the water's still deep—
the inaccessible earth, the dark birds
    in scissors cut the sky
into gray and grayer, two halves
    of the same strange atmosphere.

The trees stand up straight for now and
    the old barbecue is gone, but a whole cement
village has bricked the land over in its place.
    Every neon sign says, *Stop.*
Every market sells a season
    (poor black-capped chickadee trapped in its rafters).

The medication has made your face different,
    your skin's not the same you've lived in,
we wait at the train tracks as a new
    deluge comes, a bold blundering sky of fresh
water. (A single leaf on a tree,
    one bigleaf maple-child, a wet dog on a cement heap.)

You say you wish there was a way
    you could come back—
to find out who your wild son grows up to be,
    if the house stands up to the years of rain,
if your dear husband stands up to the years of rain.
    (A car alarm, a fire truck.)

Maybe there is a way—
　　like fish in the cold fall storms,
maybe we do, our bodies unskinned
　　and unadorned, making our way
to the place our beating belongs,
　　our pulsing light flashing up a river.

Silvery across a flooded highway,
　　our human faults forgiven, a returning to
the first uncomplicated river system,
　　blood to blood to blood, until we are carried
around in the world like one grateful fish
　　escaping the lure and seeing the same moon

it has seen for ten-thousand years,
　　the same moon our other dear fishes see,
maybe, I say (my own tenuous connection),
　　maybe, (the railroad crossing released, the car
pushing toward home) *Maybe*, I say to you,
　　Maybe we do come back.

Ways to Ease Your Animal Mind

A cloud of cormorants comes
flooding out of rushed wind,
out of sunned sea-bound waves.

The air is unwound with bird
and you are not lost in the least,
but a deliberate deserter.

Let go the oxcart.
Let go the claw and climb.

This fevered mess of world
is well-done. Lean in and nuzzle
its exceptional need to be yours.

The Commute

Your crossing guard (you call her that
although you do not employ her)
> says, *Thank God for small favors*, and the morning
> noisemakers arrive in bundles of backpack and hound.

A gray shark-like man runs with his son,
> you can tell he is pleased at his son's speed,
> you can tell he is displeased at his own.

(Time escaping, a crow in the clock,
> your beauty fading, the dates dating.)

Where's the good work? Where's the worth it?

Tony Bennett's singing now, the music never ends,
and all the men you remember have grown old.

There's the forgiving that you work so hard on,
> as if you were the lady
these babies in the school yard think you are.
Elegant lady, said a second grader as you
passed, in a hurry to stop.

(Enough of these strings and seams and corseted dresses,
> your own bones will hold you up. Even if you're held down.)

There's the school bell of shout and heart race—
> time is coming. Come into the clocked room in the skin.

Two days ago, in the shower, you said, *I'm perfectly happy.*
> Your chest muscles grown-over with river willows and nettles.

(No one believed you.)

But now, you require an answer—you want to take one.

You stand against the air and feel fist-like and wild.
You don't want clothes or shoes, you will not move.
You shove your tiny face in the world and say,
you won't go, you won't go.

Gratitude in Spite of Oneself

Cold as a coin, misery places his man-hands
on the heroine's fast-paced heart. She thinks she lacks
the pluck and nuzzle of her earlier bones, wants to give up.
Where is Northern California, why should she not
go there? Remember the butterfly tree? That strange
non-sound sound, the tongue taste of natural color, the fat
birds on trees? She is obliged to the generous authority
of the earth. She would like to thank this collection of
authentic apparitions. Thank you for coming into me,
keep me here as long as you can stand my human clutter.

The Same Thing

There's an awful story in the news.
For days you cannot sleep; it's too hot, it's too cold.

It's just a story in the news.

Not another human, not a whole country,
not another animal, just a piece of paper.

Then you feel a little better.
You go to the train and wear your headphones,
you listen to a sad song that sounds familiar.

You pass a store window and there's someone
you don't know walking where you're walking: heels,
a summer dress, hair tied up too fancy for the week.

The television says tomorrow night they will
shed some light on hell.

How far do we need to search for some bad thing?
Hell is not beneath us, not a bargaining chip with your children.

You come home on the train and you have
bought gifts and tried to be decent.

This is how your life will go, you know that. Day after day.

Awful acceptance: the soft life of your footprints.

You start to think of the alternative,
you shake your real shirt off in the hallway.

Would it be the same if you were born in Mexico? Life.
            Cuba? Ireland? 1974?

You miss everyone. Even the people you read about today
you didn't know, their faces on the brain as if on paper.

You sit on the balcony,
which is really a fire escape, but you call it
the balcony to make it sound better.
You wear the slip your grandmother gave you

fifteen years ago, the weather is nice, California nice.

You sing a little, call your family, you think, *things aren't so bad.*

You say you love the world, so love the world.

Maybe you don't even say it for yourself,
maybe you move your mouth like everyone
moves their mouth. Maybe your mouth is the same
mouth as everyone's, all trying to say the same thing.

3.

Not in the air
in the moment

—Octavio Paz

Fifteen Balls of Feathers

1.

Leaving most of the world unturned this early morning,
   I found whispered volumes in my lungs and in my ears.

What I fear most: madness, non-existence.

A hissing magnitude comes and un-houses me, only in the hours
   when I am not who I am at all.

For what seems like fifteen minutes I stare at the word "nests."
   It has too many *S*'s. It's *S* heavy. It's not a place for a bird.

All the things I've gathered seem so unlikely now, these shoes
   and this packet of seeds with no soil to live in, no drops of good sky.

My mother's psychic says, *everyone essentially wants*
the same thing as everyone else, a sense of belonging, a coming home.

I wanted to be a hummingbird.
   It made sense to long for rapid wings and the ability to hover always—

   to be Huitzilopochtli taming my snakes.

Sometimes though, the thought exhausts me and
   I want to be a slow horse, a tennis shoe.

2.

Two years ago I listened to the rain on the radiator
                    sizzle and ping into oblivion.

And I sat up in the no-account streetlight light and said,

        No one has done anything to me.

And the drops kept coming like offerings in the obedient now.

        That's true. You have done all this to yourself.

My covers were not constrictors, nor were my walls.

My elaborate constructions
            were built of stencils and explosive devices.

And in that minute I had made you all up.

Not only the lovers whose sickly pink lilies
                I had wished into sunflowers,
        but also the whiptail lizards and the live oaks
that I suspended in my spine to keep me standing,

        even the first fist-bent indiscretion, even the few people I trust, gone
to the ghostly cofferdam of my own mind.

And shit, I thought.

If madness has come to make me a make-believer,
                    then make-believe me out.

But why would I want to be so dead set,
                    so hell-bent on the actual?

Why must you exist, so I can exist?

3.

At seventeen in Darmstadt, my love was a jester on the rails,
            big blonde in the bar car he grabbed me laughing and said,

No one will ever know me. His eyes like the blinking
                        red of a junction box signal.

Outside, the fields of white asparagus made my stomach wilt.
            I was a black forest.

He was reading backward on the couchette
    while the world went by and I was
counting the faces of sunflowers. 1,753,285 yellow fools
thinking they're going to go on forever.

What numbers can you count to? How high can you go?

Infinity was a difficult concept.
                It's harder now.

4.

In the *Twilight Zone* movie where the goblin tears the plane apart,
          rips the wires out with his goblin hands, only one man
can see him. Poor mad John Lithgow sweating

          in the pale orange glow of his fantastic fear.

I like that one; the plane never goes down
          and everything's creamy and eighties cool.

Flying to my home's coast last month, I imagined that goblin
          gymnastic-ing the leading edge of the plane's wing.

Turbulence and a prayer caught coming up,
          I wanted so many things.

I took the window shade down, swallowed
          my useless story of normal life and made a list
          of things we should save our prayers for:

          the earth
          the end of war
          and more, and more.

We landed. Wished to the ground by our turbojet engines
          and navigating lights of redemption, of flight.

5.

When we passed the thin rolled-paper between our lips
    by the Wixhausen train station, we thought how funny
    the word *goods* was. How it seemed like something out of
    old movies—Peter Lorre saying, *Did you get the goods?*

The train roared by and sometimes, in flashes, we felt like we were young.
    Mostly we were high and felt as fast
    and strong as that train.

Standing on the switch point, then jumping tie to tie,
    over the fishplate bolts, the dating nail, the spikes—
    life was going on too long already.

I can see her now with her hair piled up over a flannel shirt,
        stumbling over German words and
        drinking ouzo at the Greek restaurant.

    She's not as dumb as she looks
    though she's falling headfirst into
    the eternal misunderstanding
            that trains don't stop.

6.

The very first time I really loved sex
    was the very first time I was happy to be a girl.

I found out there were two hearts in a human body.

    I stared down at my smooth stomach, its separate pounding
        crawling out my belly button like a bulldozer.

        (What a pleasure—this dual dwelling
            of mysterious punctuated pulses!)

    Lying on a cream-colored bedspread overlooking
    the plaza, I felt I had swallowed a live bird whole.

    It did not give me wings, it laid me flat out for weeks.

    I couldn't talk on the phone without shivers,
        and when I smiled, I dripped bird's blood from my gums.

We are not speaking of love,
        I birthed myself into an animal being.

7.

The last person my friend slept with before she died
          was some gorgeous stranger in Las Vegas.

We laughed about it for days
          until we didn't, and her invisible bird broke away.

      My heart's just fine,
          gravity is there, though,
          keeping me on the lure of lowdown.

      My invisible birds are still intact,
          I can open myself up and show you,
          they have muscled deep
               into an actual nest of suspended song.

8.

On the river Rhine, we watched fireworks and held tight
          with our own explosives.

I was ready to be old.

The man on the riverboat told me to take it easy.
          His broad shoulders navigating the current.

His tongue seemed too large for his mouth,
          his teeth small, like a fish's teeth.

I was too young for the captain's quarters,
                    but I demanded a woman's walk,
          a plank for the best of me.

Over the ledge I lobbed my good-luck coin
          and quick, like light in a hurry,
it slipped beneath the waves.

That was fifteen years ago.
          I'm still waiting for the river to stop right here—

          me, standing on the watery extension of time.

9.

The Aztecs believed that Huitzilopochtli's
    father was a ball of feathers.

This is true: A ball of feathers flew out of the sky and made his mother,
    Coatlicue, pregnant.

He went on to become a sun god. A fierce war god. Obsidian knife-fighter.
    His siblings, the moon and the stars.

Once upon a time, a ball of feathers . . .

    Perhaps that is how all love comes,
    unexpected and on a blast of transmogrified air.

What we define as human tenderness troubles
    each of us differently.

Legends wriggle up and we go on offering ourselves
    to the day's ordinary rituals.

Here is my sacrifice: my hummingbird landing in a stranger's palm.

10.

My mother gutted birds on the kitchen table
           and hung them up
     with black nails in her studio.

Found in Limantour's narrow spit of sand,
           or on the upended railroad ties used for garden fences,
           left there as gifts, from our white cat, Smoke.

     Tiny winged things pinned to pieces
     on the wall, feathers for a long study of flight.

What lifts us up?

She painted what flies around us, captured and still dazzled
           in the glittered air they lived so long in—

     they were crosses on the door, beasty angels of the jet stream.

     (More real than angels.)

If we define ourselves by what we study, our sordid obsessions,
     how do we hang ourselves up?

     There is no god in this bird; this bird is a god.

     Once upon a time, a ball of feathers . . .

11.

After she had been in the hospital for eight days,
     my stepmom and I sat by the tall grass under the butterfly tree.

We had broken her out successfully from tubes and torment.
     I was drinking gin at noon.

Going to the hospital is like going to the airport: Everyone does it.
     It's best to make yourself flint and stir up the scary air.

     The nurse thought I was in college and I thought, *No, I'm younger.*

I'm not sorry that I don't believe in god that way.
     (I'm sorry about a lot of things, but not that.)

One legend says that hummingbirds were sent up
     to find what was beyond the blue sky.

     (Can you imagine? Such a small thing going so far?)

     Turned out there was nothing beyond the blue sky.
     Which made the sky bluer and more holy than it had been before.

Past the lavender bushes and the big new buds of peonies,
     an orange-tailed sun-god came to welcome her home.
     Buzzing wings—within its trill there is suspension.

You know what I mean.

12.

To lay one's hand in another's without fear
      is a seemingly simple act.

The ways we affirm our own existence—focus on the bright noise
      of traffic, the blaring music of your neighbor's radio,
      the notes under the door,
      the *Do you know what I mean?*

I have been lying awake listening to the street sounds,
      which please me. The stumbling humming humans
making their ways, in the dark.

I must know that I have not dreamt you,
                that most stories are at least half true.

In one story the birds taught a woman to weave,
         in another they saved the whole world with faith.

After we came back from the doctor's office
I said to my mother,
         that perhaps now I was finally turning into a bird.

We sat in the car in the drugstore parking lot
         and took our blood pressure over and over again
until we laughed so hard the car shook.

Here's the pulse. Let's keep it forever.

13.

At the base of a bird's feather there is something called an *after-feather*.
The part that looks more like human hair in its wiry bristle.

It sounds like *afterthought* or *afterlife*. It's the part right after
the calamus
and the inferior umbilicus that goes into the bird's body.

I want one. What happens after-feather? After.

After we have accomplished the tasks assigned to us,
and eventually burst out of our names.

Don't worry, I don't believe that hummingbirds are in love with me,
no gods are ever in love with us.

The story goes that Huitzilopochtli cut off the head of his sister,
then tossed her to the sky to become the moon,
his other siblings he tossed to become the stars.

(Because there must be a great vacancy and a great way to fill it.)

My stepmom is home now and she calls
to find out how I am.

I tell her I'm sorry, and she says, *This is just the way my life is going to be.*

At the deli, the woman is so nice to me for no reason
that I start to cry.

There are times when I suppose we're supposed to rail against our lot,
other times, the moon and sun are siblings.

14.

By the banks of the river, sitting on the fat white stones
            beneath the hemlocks,

I watch her undress and slip into the current.
            She looks young. My father is quiet, and overhead
            the sun makes a point to push us closer.

            I have been memorizing things lately.

This is not a unique story—
            what we have in our hands is an unsolvable thing.

It's the passage that perplexes us,
            this full weight that must take us down.

She knows we were watching her,
            she likes to know we are there as she goes under.

15.

In every story the hummingbird is able to pass between both worlds—
        it's the messenger, the winged balancer.
The migration of so many miles beyond our earthly reach
        and still they come to us.
Carving out this pocket of air we are allotted,
                these small susurrations of wings from the other world,
                the *afterworld*,
        can keep me up at night, but pleasantly.
I know what you're thinking:

Sometimes it's the rain and the radiator,
sometimes it's the sun god.

Mostly I think of the story where the hummingbird taught
        a woman from the Tarascan tribe (my tribe) to weave.

        How she saved the hummingbird through the drought,
        how she saved the rainwater and sweetened it,
        how, in turn, the bird taught her to weave,
        how, in turn, that weaving saved her life.

4.

You've got roots cannot be torn from under
Won't you shake it like you've never done before

—The Be Good Tanyas

Bird Bound for a Good World

In the car ride to the Cape we wrought ourselves
    a radio show. My job was to keep repeating, in the voice
of a circus announcer, *Cape Cod National Seashore, step right up.*

Abraham had the job of quiet Wisconsin banter about the birds
we were bound to see now that our walls had forgiven us this.

We began a list, the easiest first:

    black-backed gull, piping plover,

We said we were the long-suffering kettle pond.
We said we were the orphans of pavement.

    cormorants, common terns, mergansers,

We said we'd like to drink whiskey when we got there.
We said, finally, we didn't love anyone and it felt wonderful.

    eiders, egrets, great blue herons,

I said I loved rocks and water and fish.
Abraham said he loved the birch woods and leaves.

    chickadees with their caps, dear, dear, sweet swallows.

We come so far from our homes,
my valley of the moon,
his Ladysmith of the woods.

And here we are, diligent birds,
trying to make a small life out of paper and string.

    Seed-hoarder, stream-nester,
warm-blooded, beak lover, bird-speaker—

go to the water, bird,
love the blue world, bird,
money means nothing, bird,
clothes mean nothing, bird,
keep going into the world, bird,
startle the sad spring air with the whirring of your wings.

Return to Rush and Flutter

You're a persistent fish swimming
the same surviving river, skinless
and unhinged by a year of bad weather.
Lost ones in the bones, your water
damage, your rage of flood and fire
and still, all along Warm Springs Road
the naked ladies have the nerve
to flower pink and full. A choir
of constant blackbirds and bees
you couldn't miss more. Go bury
your head in the wasted weeds
so you can hear the beating
deepen, the blazing suddenness
of a wound overcome by wonder.

Sharks in the Rivers II

If I moved to Santa Cruz, I could ride the roller coaster
    all the time. And learn to surf. Except for the sharks.

I admit I am hopeless.

Sharks are fish, just fish with a rubbery cartilage
        and a mind for troublemaking—stirring things up.

It's not the fish that I fear, but the jaw.
Or, it's not the jaw, it's the teeth.
It's not the teeth, but the multiple rows of teeth,
the conveyor belt of teeth growing like weeds
anchored in their shark skin.

And we think our rivers are protected,
            but what of the bull shark?
Breeding in the brackish waters of a river's mouth,
seemingly solitary, seemingly up to model
fish-like behavior.

(His tempting strength, his fluid dynamics.)

Some say a shark never sleeps, so how can I?
How can I let them into my waterless room
only to stay wide awake?

They hear me, I can tell, from miles away.

(Sharks are listening right now, I'm sending out signals.)

I'm dreaming of them. I'm wrapping my arms
around their cold, gray, magnificent bodies.

We're both sleeping
        with our shark-eyes open.

Drowning in Paradise

The low-hanging hibiscus coos out
its swollen-mouth flower song
to the rare bee holding its tongue
and I'm drunk on the bully world again—
a fueled up fluster coming on.
Look, even two oceans can collide
here in the bellies of white islands.
Splurge and risk in the conch-dark
night—I'm going to walk into the water's
frothy rim. Come here shark. Come
here barracuda. Love the sweet artifacts
of this body. Carry me in the world-class
rattle of a wave. I want the big bite, one
restless, tooth-filled mouth to take me down.

The Weather Reported

I'm glad the cabin is finished in Cañones.
        Did Elud finish the rock wall?
        The bedroom facing south?

I was less of a person then, I know.
I was less of a bird then, too.

        Do the two streams still run?
        The roadrunner? The crane?

Remember the night on the porch: Chinaco and chilies
        by the Rio Grande, the cloud that passed over us
        in the shape of your face?

We both saw it. You were the weather.

I was moving to you, to the river, but
        I was not a morning dove, or a marsh hawk.

I'm sorry that I could not stay. Your name was too big for me,
        twice my age—you were still running faster than water.

I moved to the farthest tip of the East,
        you sent me binoculars for my bird-watching,
        and a bunch of Mexican sage from the bosque.

Santiago, I am my own weather now.
Santiago, I am my own river.
Santiago, I am a better bird for flying.

Sting

Plundering deep in the moon's ring
and you enter here, unmeaning,
say, *We've got a long time ahead of us,*
a minnow's life in the current. I'm making
a list of all the things in my mouth. Bees,
and bee stings, hope. Brother, the cord
to this world is a frayed rope and it beats
our poor bodies like drum skins
and I'm running the city water now
in a sink safe from harm, and across
the surface of most states there's
a phone ringing and a somebody's lost
something, a somebody's lost a
somebody, and a somebody's come
home, and I'm unmoved in the kitchen
pulling wings out of my teeth, praying
for loads more wishes and a body
out there waiting for this somebody
in the kitchen waiting to be done stung.

The Bird Knows He Is Going to Die and Wishes Not To

She says it never matters about the blue jay on the electric wires,
        making its own electricity—saying those bright-blue things
        only a jay can say from his roost of rush and chord.

She says not to put the cart before the horse—
        the heart before the course.

But when she moves, so much light escapes.

He's squawking to all the babies now and ruffles his tail feathers like quills
        she feels more and more like a broken telephone.

This little pearl of a bird, with so much noise in him, so much to say.

(Days now, she moves her chair to the window.)

She's in love with that blue bird. She's in love with everything.

She wants to know how it works, how one word can vibrate,
        how one blue thing can scare up cobwebs and dust.

She says his name, but it's not his name at all.

Come *Danger*, come *Danger*, come *Wink*, come *Lies*.

She is wearing her changeable season, she is shedding light like feathers.

Take it easy on me, she cowers.
        But he cannot hear, he is moving too fast.

(The window closes.)

He moves the wires like an earthquake (*don't leave me*).
He squawks the jigsaw sky, he feels out of favor and out of fashion,
and here he feels again the cells in his body growing older,
the feathers unfolding, my lord he is a mortal bird.

(Falling and dying.)

Come *Blue Night*, come *Quick* and *Electric*.

The Undressing Day

I dreamed the tangled crush of magic peels
in the wax leaves made a spell of bones,
and everything bloomed big and better than
before. Beyond the barbed wire, beyond
this fence of angry fists there's a breathing,
there's a breathing underwater. Love
the body bending, the useless hair,
the *when* of the skin, the *when* of the wrist,
the witching, the *now*, the *now*, the *insist*.

To the Busted Among Us

But everyone is busted a little.

No consciousness of the breaking, just the history
of a dirty footprint—even the easy stuff,
the small conversations about our worth.

(To be an anonymous object,
the innocuous heart, the smallest part of flesh.)

On Withers Avenue, a rat circled the bottom of a trash can,
threw itself against the plastic green walls of its new world.
I heard it. I removed the top. I put the top back on.

(Small brilliant hole in the dark, let me out.)

Standing in my ridiculous human clothes,
I argued with the rat. I asked him,

Are you rabid?
Are you crazy?
Are you responsible for the plague?

He didn't answer; he threw himself again.

Are you mean?
Did you hurt your children?
Did you hurt anyone?

I want to tell you that I let that rat out,

that kindness overwhelmed the tough pout of people-cleanliness.
I want to tell you I put him in a shoe box
and brought him to the country, fed him corn and taught him to read.

(Un-gettable parallel time, fathomless choices.)

I say to a stranger, *I am harmless.*

But the word doesn't seem right. I have been harmed,
but I do not wish to do harm, but I could do harm.
(I am not without desire.)

I want to tell you the rat moved in with me, we made a good living.

But, I tell you, I let him be.

I think he might have managed to release himself,
he was not harmless. He had intent. Flirting with the world.

He'll show up one day, long-wandered in the weather.

He just needed someone subversive to bend in
real close and say,

You can rustle all you want,
you can reinvent the shout,
but you got your rat-self in there,
now, get your cunning rat-self out.

The City of Skin

Maybe it's time to get off your high horse,
             come down to the meat and bones of those
             who live below the surface,
less than hands-high,
but oh so human here.

Dive under, dive under,
bristle and thunder.

All of these failed bargains,
but god can't we agree to this—

dark comes so slowly, teeth in the hair, lips in the ears.
             What good words will do to a mouth, yes.

I'm made of a series of pulleys and string,
pull me, please, and bring
all the windowsills you've ever known.

I'll bring mine, windows open to let the fog roll.

I'm the World Fair, the rumbled-over ride,
the oxygen tank, the clatter of sun in a room,

nothing depends on the impending storm.
             I'm mum and murmur,
             a satchel of notes drawn out of the tub.

I'm past the missing and the missives and, look,

             that minnow's misbehaving!

All along this muscled kiss, this brilliant mess, yes, let's.

Big Star

Because there is so little time,
she sets her watch back, for more of everything.
Unbounded hunger for the tug of the living tree,
have mercy for this moment between fences.
She does not know how to stay unfolded
for too long in this absolute pounding. She says,
Big star, big star, bold in its opening,
bowled over in its oneness, she says, *This is the same*
hand I use for fetching what I fear, and now
I am pointing to you.

World Versus Girl

The swinging sky patterns
    itself after the inside of a giant quiver, shooting
stars at those who still cling
to the criminal bricks of their shaky morals.

Never knew a cloud to mock me so,
        an amputated tree limb pointing darkly
        at all the flaws inside my skin.

The song in my head has whiskey in it,
    and a back porch full of rusted nails in mason jars.
It sounds nothing like the song in your head.
In fact, that's the chorus.

I can hear a small angel dying on its breath.
        It was so at home there once, a nest
        of clean teeth and an honest-to-goodness tongue.

We can be our only judge, I suppose,
    but the river never runs its hands through my hair,
    never says, *Good luck, girl.*

Or at least never says it often enough.

I'm chock-full of bad ideas today,
    my foul mouth worthy of a good kick.

    Let's storm the hospital!
    Let's burn the bedsheets!

I've been walking for a long time,
    and it hasn't made me smarter or faster,
    but I bet I can still beat you.

Maybe not now, maybe not tomorrow,
but this stubborn monster-girl, gone all wrong
        with the river's sledge, is not
        giving in to your one-way-ness.

World, turn all you want to,
        faster even. I've come to like the way the breeze feels
        as it rips me limb from limb.

Fin

Tumbled in with all these sharks
swimming in the bathtub, I can't hear you anymore.

Barracuda in the blood, the coral-gossip of these good bones.

Once I said, *I wish you could pick me up at the airport.*

(Air travel: big meandering of the flesh.)

You're right here, you don't need to be picked up.

But it's what I want: the rough catch, the singular time.

How long have I been floating here?
Flickering letters in the fist, hitches in the throat.

The refrigerator says nothing; nor the window, nor the door.

Underwater all these things are swimming.
Fin of cold-blooded, spine-strong angelfish.
Fin of warm-blooded, streamlined tiger sharks.

Bathwater's full of tomorrow's spin, but still I'll hold a fat lip
kissed-dry.

Naked, I have no pocket to put you in.

Don't fall asleep in the water.
Don't fall asleep in the water.

My tenderness scared you—a circle around my scales,
the center of the universe, you said I was the center.

A smooth surface full of permission slips and please.

How many constructed conversations? Move your mouth this way.

Beguiled fish, haunted water, what's the hook now?
    (And all these nets under my arms.)

I've got the tug, I'm going under.

Gratitude goes to the editors of the following journals, in which the poems in this book first appeared:

Anti-: "The Undressing Day" and "Drowning in Paradise"

Barrelhouse: "Sharks in the Rivers" and "The Widening Road"

Barrow Street: "Big Star" and "The City of Skin"

Big Game Anthology: "Body of Rivers"

Coconut: "Homesick" and "Gratitude in Spite of Oneself"

cold-drill: "The Barer the Bones" and "Diagnosis: Even the Stillaguamish River Cannot Stop Time"

Connotation Press: "Flood Coming" and "The Weather Reported"

Diode: "Fifteen Balls of Feathers"

Effing Magazine: "Rescue Animals"

Eleven Eleven: "How to Give Up" and "Hardworking Agreement with a Wednesday"

The Fourth River: "Territory" and "The New World of Beauty"

Harvard Review: "Overjoyed"

InDigest: "Marketing Life for Those of Us Left"

La Fovea: "The Commute"

The L Magazine: "Sting"

The New Yorker: "Crush"

Octopus: "To the Busted Among Us"

Painted Bride Quarterly: "Return to Rush and Flutter"

Pleiades: "Good Girls"

Sawbuck: "High Water"

The Scrambler: "This Practice" and "The Russian River"

Subtropics: "Bird Bound for a Good World"

Big Gratitude

I am so very grateful for the love and guidance of my family and friends. They are all sorts of magic. And many thanks to the few, in particular, that read this book in different iterations: Jennifer L. Knox, Jason Schneiderman, Brady T. Brady, Stacia Brady, Trish Harnetiaux, Bryan Harnetiaux, Alex Lemon, David Doody, Nicole Hefner, Kirsten Andersen, Bob Hicok, and my editors, James Cihlar and Wayne Miller.

Notes

"Sharks in the Rivers" contains a direct quote from the *National Geographic* article sent to me by Emily Limón, "Blue Waters of the Bahamas, An Eden for Sharks," March 2007.

"Rescue Animals" was written for Rocking B Ranch in Sonoma, where my mother cares for retired police horses and unwanted farm animals.

"Not Enough" contains a direct quote from Alex Lemon. The poem was inspired by the bronze sculptures of Varda Rotem, along with the instruction from Jason Schneiderman on the Torah and Kafka.

"Territory" was written at the Emerys' Brookfarm on Sonoma Mountain.

"Marketing Life for Those of Us Left" is for, and contains quotes from, Jessica Yen, who died of cancer in August 2006.

"The Crossing" is for Cynthia Limón, who died of cancer in February 2010. It was inspired by a photograph in the local Stanwood, WA, paper, *Stanwood/Camano NEWS*.

"Ways to Ease Your Animal Mind" was written at West Wind in Stonington, CT, on dear Pam Norwood's good porch.

"The Same Thing" takes a quote from ABC's *20/20*.

"Fifteen Balls of Feathers" pulls from many online sources on Mexican, Aztec, and Tarascan myths of hummingbirds, as well as Professor Solis's course in Chicana Studies.

"Bird Bound for a Good World" contains direct quotes from Abraham Smith while we were driving on Route 6 to the Provincetown Fine Arts Work Center for a poetry reading.

Ada Limón is the twenty-fourth U.S. Poet Laureate as well as the author of *The Hurting Kind* and five other collections of poems. These include, most recently, *The Carrying*, which won the National Book Critics Circle Award and was named a finalist for the PEN/Jean Stein Book Award, and *Bright Dead Things*, which was named a finalist for the National Book Award, the National Book Critics Circle Award, and the Kingsley Tufts Award. Limón is a recipient of a Guggenheim Fellowship, and her work has appeared in the *New Yorker*, the *New York Times*, and *American Poetry Review*, among others. She is the host of American Public Media's weekday poetry podcast *The Slowdown*. Born and raised in California, she now lives in Lexington, Kentucky.

More Poetry from Milkweed Editions

To order books or for more information,
contact Milkweed at (800) 520-6455
or visit milkweed.org.

Bodega
Su Hwang

Eyes Bottle Dark with a Mouthful of Flowers
Jake Skeets

feeld
Jos Charles

Footnotes in the Order of Disappearance
Fady Joudah

The Final Voicemails
Max Ritvo

I Know Your Kind
Will Brewer

North American Stadiums
Grady Chambers

Stranger
Adam Clay

Tsunami vs. the Fukushima 50
Lee Ann Roripaugh

Vessel
Parneshia Jones

Virgin
Analicia Sotelo

Wilder
Claire Wahmanholm

milkweed
EDITIONS

Founded as a nonprofit organization in 1980, Milkweed Editions
is an independent publisher. Our mission is to identify, nurture
and publish transformative literature, and build
an engaged community around it.

Milkweed Editions is based in Bdé Óta Othúŋwe (Minneapolis)
within Mní Sota Makhóčhe, the traditional homeland of the Dakhóta
people. Residing here since time immemorial, Dakhóta people
still call Mní Sota Makhóčhe home, with four federally recognized
Dakhóta nations and many more Dakhóta people residing in what is
now the state of Minnesota. Due to continued legacies of colonization,
genocide, and forced removal, generations of Dakhóta people remain
disenfranchised from their traditional homeland. Presently, Mní
Sota Makhóčhe has become a refuge and home for many Indigenous
nations and peoples, including seven federally recognized Ojibwe
nations. We humbly encourage our readers to reflect upon the
historical legacies held in the lands they occupy.

milkweed.org

Milkweed Editions, a nonprofit publisher, gratefully acknowledges sustaining support from Emilie and Henry Buchwald; the Patrick and Aimee Butler Foundation; the Dougherty Family Foundation; the Ecolab Foundation; the General Mills Foundation; John and Joanne Gordon; William and Jeanne Grandy; the Jerome Foundation; Robert and Stephanie Karon; the Lerner Foundation; Sally Macut; Sanders and Tasha Marvin; the McKnight Foundation; Mid-Continent Engineering; the Minnesota State Arts Board, through an appropriation by the Minnesota State Legislature, a grant from the Wells Fargo Foundation Minnesota, and a grant from the National Endowment for the Arts; Kelly Morrison and John Willoughby; the National Endowment for the Arts, and the American Reinvestment and Recovery Act; the Navarre Corporation; Ann and Doug Ness; Jörg and Angie Pierach; the RBC Foundation USA; Ellen Sturgis; the Target Foundation; the James R. Thorpe Foundation; the Travelers Foundation; Moira and John Turner; and Edward and Jenny Wahl.

MINNESOTA
STATE ARTS BOARD

NATIONAL
ENDOWMENT
FOR THE ARTS
A great nation
deserves great art.

TARGET.

THE McKNIGHT FOUNDATION

Interior design by Connie Kuhnz
Typeset in Minion Pro
by Bookmobile Design & Digital Publisher Services
Printed on acid-free 100% post consumer waste paper
by Kingery Printing